Warner Bros. presents

my FaiR LaDY

"Look at her,
a pris'ner
of the
gutters..."

Jack L. Warner, producer of
"My Fair Lady" and president
of Warner Bros. Pictures.

"My Fair Lady"... A Milestone for Jack L. Warner

The far-reaching influence and colorful personality of Jack L. Warner have made a lasting mark on the world of motion picture entertainment.

For a half century he has looked upon the screen as the most potent, most exciting and most rewarding expression of show business. Through the screen's tumultuous history from shaky silents to richly resonant stereophonic sound—or from "My Four Years in Germany" to "My Fair Lady"—he has played a dominating role.

With "My Fair Lady," Jack Warner has personally achieved the greatest triumph in his company's history.

In the past as president of Warner Bros. Pictures, his hand has been felt in all the company's enterprises, and on several occasions he has served as a supervising producer. But in the case of "My Fair Lady," he took on the job of being its very active, very dedicated and very enthusiastic producer.

From the night he first saw the New York stage performance of "My Fair Lady" early in its long run, he was captured with the conviction that herein lay the motion picture of all time, and he was resolved to bring it to the screen as a personal production for his company.

The record $5,500,000 which he paid for the property and which rocked an industry unprepared for such a courageous gesture of economic confidence, was regarded by Warner as a sound and reasonable investment.

He backed up this investment with the talents of the finest artists and craftsmen to be found in the motion picture industry today, and with the most advanced techniques of sight and sound on the screen.

The result is a milestone in entertainment, one widely applauded by the entire film industry and one designed to bring a new and exhilarating theatre experience to people all over the world.

Wilfrid Hyde-White   J. L. Warner   Audrey Hepburn   Rex Harrison
George Cukor

The Shining World of My Fair Lady...

The Warner Bros. motion picture presentation of "My Fair Lady" is a dazzling climax to a magic success story. The $17,000,000 production offers glittering evidence of two years of painstaking effort and loving care. It has been aimed at the achievement of perfection in every department—a visual, dramatic, musical and technical perfection never before believed possible on the screen.

Most of all, it has been created by Warner Bros. and the many other artists involved, to bring audiences the rich rewards of being joyously and movingly entertained.

From the 1912 year of its birth in the play "Pygmalion" by George Bernard Shaw (that waspish source of wit, intellectual energy and controversy) to its wondrous musical form, as introduced by Alan Jay Lerner and Frederick Loewe to the New York stage in 1956, "My Fair Lady" has never been anything less than a hit.

The motion picture was personally produced by Jack L. Warner, president of Warner Bros. Pictures and a man who was willing to throw the full financial and talent resources of his company into making "My Fair Lady" a classic of the screen.

It was directed by George Cukor, a distinguished veteran of the Hollywood scene and a man whose taste and eloquent understanding of the motion picture in all its entertainment aspects have never been surpassed.

The radiant talents of Audrey Hepburn and the slick magnetism of Rex Harrison are conjoined to give the screen an unforgettable Eliza Doolittle, who starts in tatters and violets and ends in knowing splendor, and an equally unforgettable Henry Higgins, the outrageously inconsiderate professor and yet a most human man who really does grow accustomed to her face.

Better perhaps than any other Shaw work, this motion picture reflects the lyrical excitement of his characters, their high spirits and explosive indignation. The disinterested conceit of Higgins, his disregard for Eliza, and her rebellion against his high-handed self-absorption—not to mention Alfred P. Doolittle's bewilderment as one of the undeserving poor who finds himself up against middle-

G.B.S.   Technicians behind the Ascot Scene.

class morality—are Shavian delights which director Cukor has illuminated with affection.

As a film production, "My Fair Lady" is opulent in detail just as it is eye-filling in the overall lushness of SuperPanavision 70 and Technicolor.

From the panache of ostrich on an Ascot hat to the etched brass doorknobs in Higgins' study, Cecil Beaton, production, scenery and costume designer, has indulged the picture with an unprecedented richness.

The Oriental carpets in Higgins' home were re-dyed to achieve color harmony; the lampshades, wallpaper, Edwardian bric-a-brac, and the Art Nouveau furnishings of Mrs. Higgins' home were hand-picked or hand-made or in many cases imported from London. The stained glass windows were done by specially trained artisans, the handsomely carved staircase is made of rich oak; the cage for the mynah bird is a $1250 collector's piece and the Ascot silver service is priceless.

Mr. Beaton designed a total of 1,086 costumes, whose cost went beyond the $500,000 mark. And more than $1,000,000 was expended on the sets, which at one time during the production, occupied a majority of the 26 Warner Studio sound stages.

Most spectacular of the sets is probably Ascot Park, where 300 extravagantly gowned ladies and smartly tailored men perform the Ascot Gavotte. The styling and costumery of the sequence, with its deceptively simple balance and design in black, white and grey, backlighted in glaring white light, is a never-to-be-forgotten sight.

Even the atmosphere players were hand-picked by Mr. Cukor, who chose statuesque model types for the opera and ballroom ladies (preferably of six-foot height and with 24-inch waists), and members of the Londoners' and Troupers' clubs and various Scottish clans for the Covent Garden market scenes.

In the biggest operation of its kind in Warner history, Stage 3 was turned into a wardrobe and makeup factory for the Ascot Races and the Embassy Ball. Thirty-five hairdressers, 26 makeup men and 17 wardrobe women took care of the 150 women who participated in the scenes.

For the preparation of the gowns for the opera, Ascot and ballroom, 93 seamstresses, drapers, sewers and milliners worked for six months before production was begun.

The graceful music of Frederick Loewe and the infectious lyrics of Alan Jay Lerner (who also wrote the book and the screenplay) established "My Fair Lady" as a once-in-a-lifetime hit when it opened on the stage in New York in March, 1956. Six and one-half years (and 2,717 performances) later, it closed a record engagement in September, 1962.

The screen music for "My Fair Lady" was recorded in six-track stereophonic sound, the highest grade possible in the perfection of recording and engineering techniques. The wonderfully rich effects give the audience the impression of listening to a "live" orchestra and "live" voices. Five loudspeakers are placed behind the screen, and the sixth track feeds loudspeakers placed throughout the auditorium.

All this is the shining world of "My Fair Lady."

The Shining
World of
My Fair Lady...

"Who takes
good care
of me; oh,
wouldn't
it be
loverly?"

The Genius of L & L...

The stunning collaboration of Alan Jay Lerner and Frederick Loewe for "My Fair Lady" elevated these highly gifted men to a place where they were acclaimed the best writer-composer team in the American musical theatre.

High acclaim, indeed. Yet aside from the immediate popular acceptance of the "Fair Lady" music, the high quality of their work, the durability of the songs and their international appeal have shown conclusively that Lerner and Loewe brought something to the musical theatre that may never be matched.

Who else but Alan Lerner could have written: *"A pensive man am I/Of philosophic joys/Who likes to medi-tate/Contemplate/Free from humanity's mad, inhuma. noise . . ."?*

And who else but Frederick Loewe could have set to enchanting music the petulant indignation of a phonetic: professor trying to justify his eccentricities by proclaiming that he's just an ordinary man?

In their collaborative work, Lerner came up with the song title and usually the first line (avoiding, inci dentally, 's' sounds), after which Loewe took over and started putting the music together. Lerner's lyrics have been described as being like expertly cut glass, while Loew thinks of music in terms of color.

The Lerner-Loewe union began more than 20 year. ago with a show called "The Life of the Party," which the

wrote in 12 days and which ran for nine weeks in Detroit. Their first Broadway production was "What's Up?" presented in 1943, followed two years later by "The Day Before Spring," which ran for five months. "Brigadoon" appeared in 1947 and "Paint Your Wagon" in 1951. The tremendous success of "My Fair Lady" in 1956 was followed by another great success in "Camelot."

Lerner wrote the screenplay of "An American in Paris," for which he won an Academy Award, and Lerner and Loewe joined talents for the motion picture, "Gigi," for which they won three Oscars between them.

Their twinship ends with the melding of their words and music—for, as men, they represent, as do all men, distinct personalities. Reared in a Park Avenue apartment (his father founded the chain of apparel stores that bears the family name), Lerner is self-contained, mannered and fastidious. He is witty, elusive and social. His Manhattan office is, or was, embellished with a Ben Shahn painting of a bird, and a handsome Chinese horse.

Loewe was born to the musical theatre in Vienna. His father, Edmond, a tenor, was the first Prince Danilo in "The Merry Widow" and the first Chocolate Soldier in Berlin. His mother, Rose, was an actress. Loewe is given to emotion and flamboyance. He is, he says, too old to be modest; therefore, he is willing to acknowledge his genius. Presently, he lives in sand-duned splendor in Palm Springs, the sequined resort whose charities the Loewe purse has greatly enriched.

"With a little bit, with a little bit, with a little b

bloomin' luck!"

A Touch of Cukor...

It was probably inevitable that George Cukor would direct "My Fair Lady."

His long experience, his enviable record of accomplishment on the screen and his background of taste and vitality made Cukor the ideal man for the year's most important directorial undertaking.

For him, "My Fair Lady" was a year-long artistic indulgence, a happy and challenging year, and a rewarding one. "I went about putting this musical play on film with a determination to make it as perfect as a man-made, talent-inspired thing can be," he says.

There wasn't a detail too small for the director to overlook, whether it was a sly glance from Audrey Hepburn, an irascible groan from Rex Harrison, a crystal chandelier, an Edwardian flower vase, a cockney's shoelace, a musical note or an extra's moustache.

At the same time, drawing on his consummate knowledge of the theatre and his scholarly approach to Bernard Shaw, the director was continuously aware of the obligation he held to the millions of people who cherish "My Fair Lady" both as Shaw's "Pygmalion" and as a brilliant musical show.

"Jack Warner and I wanted to keep the film moving so that it would never become static like a photographed play," he says. "At the same time, I didn't want to let it burst the bounds of what 'Fair Lady' did on the stage. I wanted to capture the style of the Broadway production, with its wit married to its music. Shaw must never be slighted. But above all, I always kept in mind that this is a movie, that we must take advantage of all the splendid technical and creative scope that the screen has given us."

George Cukor's fierce dedication to the making of "My Fair Lady" exploded in a turmoil of activity that would have felled a lesser man. Before the picture started, the director visited London to explore the backgrounds, compiled 18 fat notebooks of research material, talked to hundreds of people about the show, and immersed himself so deeply in "My Fair Lady" and all its heady aspects that he was completely dominated by his work.

He plunged from "book" rehearsals with the principals to sessions with Cecil Beaton on colors and textures; then to Hermes Pan's dance rehearsals, recording sessions with Andre Previn, back to work out with Rex Harrison the intricacies of the phonetics machines. He checked the tone and design of Higgins' parlor wallpaper, refused to compromise with artificial violets for Audrey Hepburn's flower basket, conferred with diction experts on the authenticity of the cockney accent, with British experts on court presentation procedures, with jugglers on basket balancing, and he rejected one grenadier uniform in favor of another.

And most importantly, he outlined imaginative cinema extensions of this, the most famous musical of all time, and thus he spearheaded a project destined to make motion picture history, as well as Cukor history.

The director's well ordered mind, infinite patience and wide-angle talents kept everything in focus. He has enormous resources of creativity, concentration and dramatic insight. He is, indeed, one of the screen's great artists.

"My Fair Lady" is the 47th motion picture Cukor has directed in a career that spans 34 years. Within the framework of those years he has explored almost every subject and guided almost every important star. It would be impossible to name his most successful picture before "My Fair Lady"—but surely among his best are "A Bill of Divorcement," "Dinner at Eight," "Little Women," "David Copperfield," "Camille," "The Women," "The Philadelphia Story," "Gaslight," "A Double Life," "Born Yesterday" and "A Star Is Born."

He has molded great acting careers, established trends and has unfailingly worked toward the lifting of entertainment standards. "My Fair Lady" is towering evidence of the quality of his work.

"I'm an
ordinary man..."

An EXTRAordinary Man...

As suave as a velvet lapel, as elegant as a prime minister and as skillful as a prestidigitator, Rex Harrison has created in Professor Higgins a character with the enduring aura of immortality.

His tremendous success with Higgins has been attributed mostly, of course, to his vast resources of talent, but partly, too, to his unclouded view of the role of a man who may be very much like himself.

"I find it less difficult than some actors," Harrison was once quoted as saying, "to be irascible without being unpleasant." It is a quotation worthy of application to Higgins, whose self-concern makes his behavior as inconsiderate as Eliza's lack of education makes her. Higgins may be rude, but his rudeness is indiscriminating. He treats everybody alike.

With this "My Fair Lady," Harrison has played Higgins for the 1,007th, and presumably the last, time.

He appeared in "My Fair Lady" for two years on the New York stage, and one year in London. After a lapse of almost four years, when he went on to other noble things, he came to Warner Bros. for the film enactment, and decided that he had to get to know this man all over again.

"I approached the film performance with some slight misgivings," he says. "Most of all, I didn't want to warm over a role that had been such a rewarding one to me—and I hope to many other people. I faced the danger of losing the vitality and freshness that it needed. My fears could have been allayed because, from the start of rehearsal, I made the happy discovery that familiarity with the part remained an asset, and that the new and exciting medium into which Higgins was now entering would assure his vigor and freshness."

Harrison admits that Higgins is the same person he was in the theatre, "but on the sound stages I tried to achieve the same effect in a different manner. I suppose subtlety is the keynote of the screen. In the theatre, everything must be projected; but the camera and the microphone clutch onto every nuance of voice or gesture on film. It is the difference between addressing a convention and conversing with friends."

As a most admired performer, Harrison walks alone. Everywhere, his talent has earned respect and considerable awe. Although, even to the end of "My Fair Lady," Professor Higgins never really understands Eliza, at least he gets a glimmer of what life might be without her, and as a result, he takes the first faltering step toward enlightenment. And therein, of course, lies the great difference between Harrison and Higgins. Harrison has long been an enlightened actor, personality, and man.

"By George, she's got it!"

She's Really Got It!...

Since it appears that "My Fair Lady" is destined to become a modern screen classic, then Audrey Hepburn has drawn the choice motion picture assignment of many years, and one perfectly attuned to her artistry.

As Eliza Doolittle, the cockney flower girl described by Professor Higgins as "so deliciously low, so horribly dirty," she becomes, under his persistent, scowling and aggravating tutelage, a captivating princess.

And Audrey Hepburn is truly a princess. In the star-spangled history of Hollywood, no other actress has held herself so highly. Her poise has never been known to waver. Her reputation as an actress and as a woman has never been challenged. She has never been out of step, and her professionalism and principles have remained strong. So have her fans.

She looks upon "My Fair Lady" as the most rewarding, the most important and the most challenging picture she has ever done. "It was an enchanting, a once-in-a-lifetime experience," she says, somewhat breathlessly. Producer Jack Warner and Director

George Cukor gave this star the professional workout of her life. "In Miss Hepburn's character," Cukor explains, "I tried to show her as Shaw originally conceived Eliza: her father's daughter, wild and untrammeled. Her intelligence must become manifest slowly and she must realize she is up against an extremely complicated as well as an intelligent man in Professor Higgins."

Miss Hepburn started developing her interpretation of Eliza long before the picture began, and she worked for six weeks with a vocal coach, with the dance director, the musical director, and posed for endless hours in Cecil Beaton gowns.

"I believe this is the most difficult characterization I've ever undertaken," she says. "In some ways, Eliza is the first real character I've attempted on the screen. In others there has almost always been a little bit of me; in this one, there is none."

Thus she discounts, for some reasons known only to herself, such remarkable Hepburn characterizations as Sister Luke in "The Nun's Story" and Holly Golightly in "Breakfast at Tiffany's" and her Academy Award performance in "Roman Holiday."

Although she has never been anything less than an elegant lady herself, she found herself at the bottom of the ladder of femininity in the first part of "My Fair Lady." As the scroungy, unkempt Eliza of London's gutters, she underwent the horrors of having her hair heavily vaselined and thickened with fuller's earth. Her hands were purposely soiled, grime under the fingernails. She succumbed, however, to one gesture of sweet femininity in overt defiance of Eliza. She doused herself bountifully with perfume—an inconsistency nobody can see but that the crew could savor.

In Beaton's fantastic gowns, Miss Hepburn does indeed emerge as the grandest lady in all London. She wears her own beauty and grace to complement the splendor of Beaton's designs. "He makes you look the way you have always wanted to look," she says.

George Cukor has remarked that all actresses should take lessons in manners from Audrey Hepburn. She never turns in anger. Although she always has ideas of her own, she will listen with reason and is willing to compromise. She has a deeply ingrained sense of duty, whether it is toward her home, her work, or the press. "I always try to do what seems right," she says.

And what seems exactly right is her performance of Eliza Doolittle, a glowing and magnetic performance that will endure as long as the memory of George Bernard Shaw himself.

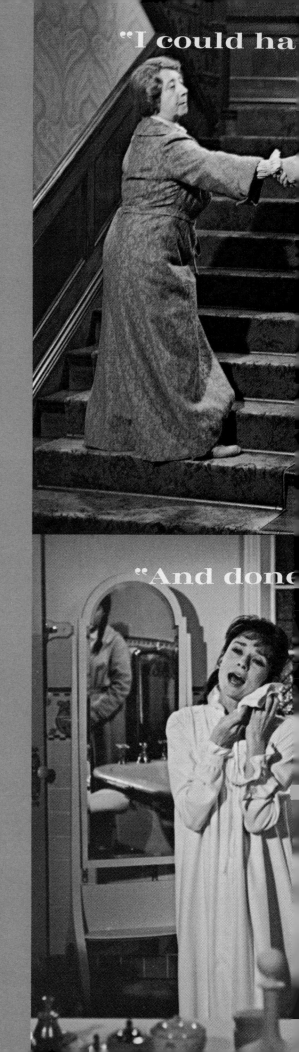

"I could
have danced
all night...

"I could ha

"And don

read my wings...

ousand things...

"I've never done before."

Tatters and Violets...

The artistry of Cecil Beaton, a famous man of plural distinctions, has given "My Fair Lady" an enrichment unrivalled in film-making.

Beaton was production, scenery and costume designer, an assignment calculated to encompass almost everything visual, ranging from the Art Nouveau decor of Mrs. Higgins' home to the texture and styling of Eliza Doolittle's ballgown.

Jack L. Warner was fully aware of the artistry of Beaton, who had designed the costumes for both the New York and London stage productions of "My Fair Lady," so he was summoned to the studio well buttressed for the wide-ranging complexities of the undertaking. Beaton is, among other things, an acknowledged authority on Edwardian elegance.

The grey respectability of the Covent Garden set, the musty Victorian masculinity of Professor Higgins' Wimpole Street home (patterned in essence, Beaton says, after his own doctor's home in London), the opulence of the Embassy ballroom, the breathtaking costumery of Ascot, and the authentic tattiness of the costermongers are among the infinity of details to which Beaton was dedicated.

For the more than 1000 costumes which he designed for the picture, Beaton resorted to all the extravagant embellishments possible in the world of fashion—such as opera capes fringed with feathers, in lamé, in zebra skin, in patterned velvet, gowns with beads and sequins and ermine tails and taffeta roses and organdy boas.

Hundreds of yards of fabric were unfolded for the Ascot scenes—many of them imported from heaven-knows-where. The Ascot is in black and white and grey, with a few square inches of alabaster flesh showing among the ladies. The 130 men in grey morning coats, top hats, Ascot (what else?) ties and spats, carry binoculars and swing canes. The event takes place in front of huge latticed pavilions with striped canvas tops, ornamented with enormous baskets of lavender hydrangeas, in the middle of 2500 square yards of lush green carpeting.

The central figure of the Ascot frolic is, of course, Audrey Hepburn, in her first flush of instant glamor. Her gown is the costliest, her hat the flashiest, her bearing the most regal and that single red flower the reddest.

It should be noted, too, that Eliza's look of bedragglement as the flower girl was not easy to come by. The antiquation of her black velvet jacket, for instance, took two weeks. As for Rex Harrison's outfits, the job was simple. His suits and sweaters were steamed to give them the classic baggy, unpressed look of an English bachelor.

Beaton has frequently photographed the British Royal Family. So too, between "races" on the Ascot set, he found time to make handsome camera portraits of Miss Hepburn and Mr. Harrison and other principals of "My Fair Lady."

"Knowing I'm on the street where you live."

DY MY FAIR LADY MY
R LADY MY FAIR LADY
AIR LADY MY FAIR LADY
MY FAIR

"What a
gripping,
absolutely
ripping
moment..."

"Tonight, old man, you did i

Andre Did It! Andre Previn,

a young and creative man, has contributed bountifully to the musical culture of motion pictures. As supervisor and conductor of the music for "My Fair Lady," he was charged with the responsibility of making a great score even greater.

All of Previn's energies have been channeled into the world of music, and his association with "My Fair Lady" gives him new stature and distinction in a field he has already conquered.

He leads more than a half dozen musical lives and excels in all of them. He is a classical and jazz pianist, a composer of serious and popular music, writer of background music for nearly 40 films, arranger, recording artist and conductor.

He has been nominated 11 times for an Academy Award and has won three Oscars.

He is highly articulate, with a range of interests extending far beyond classical, film or jazz music, and he has scored dozens of important motion pictures. And his recording of the music for "My Fair Lady" several years ago became one of the best-selling jazz albums of all time.

Hermes Did It! The classical

stylishness of the Embassy Ball, the arrogant struts of the Ascot Gavotte and the abandoned frivolity of the flower market were the inspiration of Hermes Pan.

He was choreographer for "My Fair Lady," an undertaking that drew him deeper into the movement and animation of the film than mere dance steps.

Hermes led Audrey Hepburn up the stairway and to bed as she sang "I Could Have Danced All Night"; he led Stanley Holloway and cohorts through the London slums and pubs for "Get Me to the Church on Time," and he led Miss Hepburn, Rex Harrison and Wilfrid Hyde-White into the unrestrained romping of "The Rain in Spain."

Hermes Pan, born Hermes Panagiotopulos, started his dance direction with "Flying Down to Rio," Fred Astaire's first starring picture. Pan stayed with Astaire through many musicals, and in his career has become one of Hollywood's most renowned dance directors.

WILLIAM ZIEGLER is one of the most highly respected film editors in motion pictures. His work at Warner Bros. has brought him two Academy Award nominations— one for "Auntie Mame" and the other for "The Music Man." During his 30 years in his craft, Ziegler has served with most of the leading film-makers. For the last 15 years he has been engaged at Warner Bros. Studios.

They All Did It!

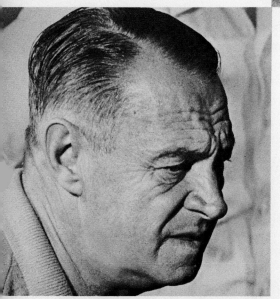

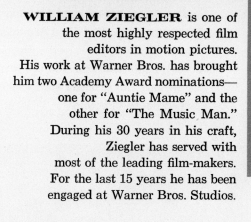

HARRY STRADLING, one of the screen's most distinguished cameramen, was director of photography for "My Fair Lady." Stradling is a veteran of more than 300 feature films (among them Leslie Howard's "Pygmalion"). He is an 11-time Academy Award nominee, and the winner of an Oscar in 1945.

GEORGE GROVES has been
a leading technician and a creative
craftsman in the development of
sound motion pictures since their
inception. He has long been affiliated
with Warner Bros.
Groves was responsible for the high
quality of perfection in the six-track
stereophonic sound reproduction
heard in "My Fair Lady."
Groves supervised the scoring and sound
effects for "Don Juan," with which
Warner Bros. introduced sound
almost 40 years ago.

?DON BAU Head of
?er Bros.' makeup department,
?n Bau supervised the enormous
?p job for "My Fair Lady." At one
?e had 26 makeup men busy
?ng faces and outlining eyebrows.
?eveloped a new luminous
?p for the "Fair Lady" players.
?es the ladies of the show a
?den look," in keeping with the
?rdian complexions of 50 years ago.

GENE ALLEN has been
associated with director George Cukor
for many years. While he was the
art director for "My Fair Lady,"
he was also Cukor's good right hand
and was of infinite assistance
to the director.

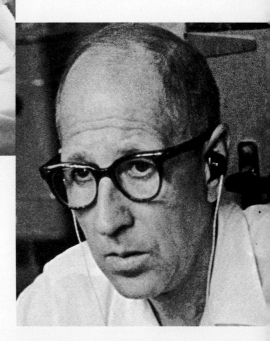

FRANCIS J. SCHEID The man
behind the complex sound equipment is
Francis J. Scheid, the sound recorder
who kept his finely tuned ear on the
voices and music of "My Fair Lady."
It was Scheid who operated the
electronics equipment which allowed
Rex Harrison, with hidden microphones,
to sing his songs "live."

"Pull out the
stopper,
Let's have
a whopper,
But get me
to the church
on time!"

STANLEY HOLLOWAY. The role of Alfred P. Doolittle, one of George Bernard Shaw's most delightful characters, must belong everlastingly to Stanley Holloway.

This artful comedian of the English music halls played Doolittle in the New York and London stage productions of "My Fair Lady" for three and a half years. Nothing, he says, could have lured him to continue the role—nothing, that is, except an offer to repeat it in the Warner Bros. motion picture.

His cheerful performance of "With a Little Bit of Luck" and "Get me to the Church on Time" are cherished moments in the musical theatre. And his skilled characterization of the dustman constantly at odds with middle-class morality would have pleased GBS himself.

Between the conclusion of his "Fair Lady" stage capers and the film, Holloway was the star of a television series, "Our Man Higgins." Years ago in England he also created the famous "Sam Small" character who became a cartoon favorite throughout the British Empire.

Holloway is one comedian, he says of himself, who does not yearn to play Hamlet. He appeared in the play once, however, enacting a comedy role to Sir Laurence Olivier's Hamlet.

WILFRID HYDE-WHITE. Wifrid Hyde-White, the redoubtable British actor, so polished, so eloquent, has been a success on the London and New York stages and in British and American motion pictures for more than a quarter of a century.

When he came to Warner Bros., he brought from London his American wife, his two young children, his 25-year-old umbrella (black, of course) and his brand-new maroon Rolls-Royce, and he stayed to bring new style to the role of Colonel Pickering in "My Fair Lady."

Hyde-White attended the Royal Academy of Dramatic Art in London, where, he slyly reports, he learned two things: (1) that he had absolutely no dramatic ability and (2) that even without it, a man could still be a success as an actor.

He recalls that, when he was a student at the Royal Academy, George Bernard Shaw visited a rehearsal. In a burst of enthusiasm, young Hyde-White asked the master's advice on reading lines. Shaw's reply: "Read them, young man, as I expect all of my lines to be read... in such a manner that people in the audience will nudge one another and exclaim: "Only George Bernard Shaw could have written those lines!"

GLADYS COOPER. The glamorous young woman in the painting above the mantelpiece in Professor Higgins' study is Gladys Cooper. It was made when she was the toast of the British Empire in the days of World War I.

And it belongs above the professor's mantelpiece because Miss Cooper plays Henry Higgins' mother in "My Fair Lady," and she plays it with the vigor and style that have characterized her work for many years.

During the time she was London's reigning stage beauty Miss Cooper's photographs were everywhere. Her endorsement of beauty aids assured tremendous sales, and long lines of Ivors, Ians, Noels and Vyvyans queued up nightly at her stagedoor

In 1922 the actress triumphed in a revival of "The Second Mrs. Tanqueray." The first night audience included the King and Queen and the Prince of Wales. She still treasures the note King George sent backstage: "You are even better than Mrs. Patrick Campbell in this part."

Miss Cooper came to Hollywood in 1940 with Sir Gerald DeMaurier for a role in "Rebecca." This was the first of many motion pictures in which she appeared. She received an Academy Award for her performance in "Now, Voyager."

THEODORE BIKEL. "Oozing charm from ev'ry pore, he oiled his way around the floor." That's Professor Higgins' description of Zoltan Karpathy, the Hungarian who tries to prove Eliza a fraud.

Theodore Bikel, who describes himself a general practitioner in the world of entertainment, plays Karpathy in "My Fair Lady." He was born in Vienna, grew up in Israel and succeeded in England and America.

Besides Bikel the actor, there is also Bikel the folk singer-guitarist, who is in constant demand on the concert stage and who has a song repertoire in 17 languages. There is also Bikel the recording artist. And Bikel the author.

He first gained fame as an actor in London in the role of Mitch in "A Streetcar Named Desire," followed by "The Love of Four Colonels." He appeared on Broadway in "Tonight in Samarkand" and "The Rope Dancers," and opposite Mary Martin in "The Sound of Music," in which he played for two years.

JEREMY BRETT. Jeremy Brett, a shiny, clear-eyed young Englishman, abandoned the London theatre to come to Hollywood and play Freddie Eynsford-Hill in "My Fair Lady."

This is the callow young man who becomes extravagantly devoted to Eliza Doolittle and who sings "On the Street Where You Live" in pursuit of his affections, and who almost, but not quite, marries the girl.

To appear in "My Fair Lady," Jeremy made his first trip to the U.S. West Coast, where he found the vegetables in the super-markets "looked like oil paintings."

Jeremy is mannerly and thoughtful; he has humor and a buoyant spirit, and he won his role of Freddie in "My Fair Lady" over some 40 other shiny young Englishmen.

MONA WASHBOURNE. Mona Washbourne is one of the best known character women in the British theatre. She was leading lady to Sir Laurence Olivier in "Semi-Detached" and toured with Noel Coward in "Nude With Violin" and "Present Laughter."

She came to Hollywood at the invitation of George Cukor to play the role of Rex Harrison's housekeeper, Mrs. Pearce, in "My Fair Lady."

Looking back on her career, Miss Washbourne says that mother didn't know best as far as this daughter was concerned. "Mother was a conservative Victorian figure," the actress says. "She rigidly disapproved of the theatre. At best she considered acting a trivial profession, and at worst she believed it to be an immoral one."

When the maternal permission finally came, Miss Washbourne reports, "I remember crying through sheer joy."

She made her London debut in a small role in Eugene O'Neill's "Mourning Becomes Electra." Ever since then, she has been happy and successful in her work.

ISOBEL ELSOM. To Isobel Elsom comes the distinction of speaking the first lines in "My Fair Lady." She emerges from the Opera House, along with scores of others, dressed in Cecil Beaton's best. "Don't stand there, Freddie. Go find me a cab. Do you want me to catch pneumonia?," says Miss Elsom, huddled with her ridiculous son, Freddie, under the portico of St. Paul's as the rain—2500 gallons of it per minute, as a matter of fact—pelts down on Covent Garden and scatters the flower-mongers.

Miss Elsom, Cambridge-born and stage-reared in London, plays Mrs. Eynsford-Hill, one of the "swells." She first came to the Hollywood screen in 1941 to star in "Ladies in Retirement." She has also appeared in "Between Two Worlds," and many other important pictures.

"You, dear friend, who talks so well,
You can go to Hartford,
Heresford and Hampshire!"

"I've grown accustomed to her face..."

Warner Bros. Pictures

presents

MY FAIR LADY

Technicolor®   Super Panavision® 70

The Cast

Starring

| AUDREY HEPBURN | Eliza |
| REX HARRISON | Henry Higgins |

Co-Starring

STANLEY HOLLOWAY	Alfred Doolittle
WILFRID HYDE-WHITE	Colonel Pickering
GLADYS COOPER	Mrs. Higgins
JEREMY BRETT	Freddie

and

| THEODORE BIKEL | Zoltan Karpathy |

with

MONA WASHBOURNE	Mrs. Pearce
ISOBEL ELSOM	Mrs. Eynsford-Hill
JOHN HOLLAND	Butler

Production

Produced by	Jack L. Warner
Directed by	George Cukor
Screenplay by	Alan Jay Lerner

(Based upon the musical play as produced on the stage by Herman Levin,
Book and Lyrics by Alan Jay Lerner, Music by Frederick Loewe)

From a play by	Bernard Shaw
Director of Photography	Harry Stradling, A.S.C.
Costumes, Scenery & Production Designed by	Cecil Beaton
Art Director	Gene Allen
Film Editor	William Ziegler
Sound by	Francis J. Scheid and Murray Spivack
Lyrics by	Alan Jay Lerner
Music by	Frederick Loewe
Music Supervised and Conducted by	Andre Previn
Additional Music by	Frederick Loewe
Vocal Arrangements by	Robt. Tucker
Orchestrations by	Alexander Courage, Robert Franklyn, Al Woodbury
Choreography by	Hermes Pan
Unit Manager	Sergei Petschnikoff
Set Decorator	George James Hopkins
Makeup Supervisor	Gordon Bau, SMA
Supervising Hair Stylist	Jean Burt Reilly, C.H.S.
Assistant Director	David Hall